GYMNASTICS
by Jason Page

Good Teamwork
Russian gymnasts are shown here celebrating their victory in the team event at the 1996 Olympic Games in Atlanta, USA.

GYMNASTIC EVENTS

Gymnastics is one of only five sports that have been included in every single modern Olympics — the others are athletics, swimming, fencing and cycling.

SUPER STATS

In 1976, 18,000 spectators watched the final of the women's individual combined events — the biggest crowd ever at an Olympic gymnastics event. If all these people stood on each other's shoulders, they would be 3.5 times as tall as Mount Everest!

NAKED TRUTH

Soldiers in ancient Greece were taught gymnastics as part of their military training. In fact, the word 'gymnastics' comes from the Greek word *gymnos* which means naked, because in ancient times all gymnasts performed in the nude! To find out what gymnasts will be wearing at the Olympic Games in Sydney turn to pages 12, 14 and 15.

Dancers depicting ancient Greek athletes, Centennial Olympic Games

DIFFERENT DISCIPLINES

There will be three different kinds of gymnastic events at the Games in Sydney. They are known as the three 'disciplines' of gymnastics and are called: artistic gymnastics, rhythmic gymnastics and trampoline. The trampoline is a new event which will appear for the very first time at the Olympic Games in 2000.

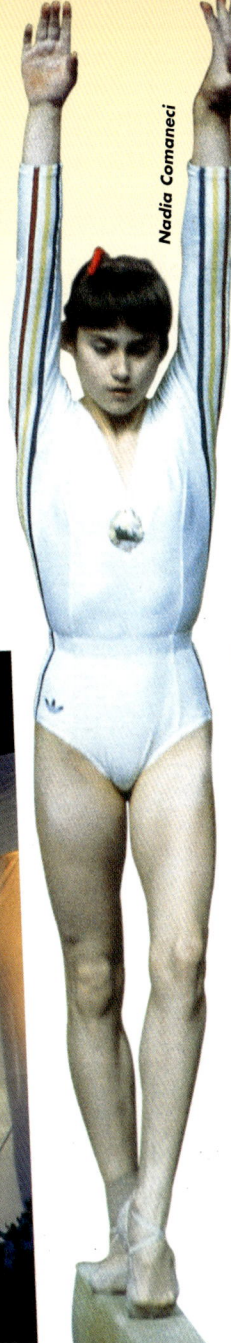
Nadia Comaneci

SEVEN OF THE BEST

At the Games in 1976, 14-year-old Nadia Comaneci (ROM) became the first person in Olympic history ever to score a 'perfect 10', the highest score possible in a gymnastic event. But she didn't just do it once — she went on to produce no less than seven perfect performances. However, the score boards couldn't cope and her perfect 10 scores had to be displayed as 1.00!

OLYMPICS FACT FILE

🎽 The Olympic Games were first held in Olympia, in ancient Greece, around 3,000 years ago. They took place every four years until they were abolished in AD 393.

🎽 A Frenchman called Pierre de Coubertin (1863–1937) revived the Games, and the first modern Olympics were held in Athens in 1896.

🎽 The modern Games have been held every four years since 1896, except in 1916, 1940 and 1944, due to war. Special 10th-anniversary Games took place in 1906.

🎽 The symbol of the Olympic Games is five interlocking coloured rings. Together, they represent the five different continents from which athletes come to compete.

MODERN GYMNASTICS

The first modern gymnastic equipment was designed and built by a German school teacher named Friedrich Jahn in the early 1800s. The sport soon caught on in schools and athletic clubs, and its popularity ensured that it was included in the first-ever modern Olympic Games. Women competed in gymnastic events at the Olympics for the first time in 1928.

ARTISTIC EVENTS

The difference between the artistic events and the other gymnastic events is that they are performed on *apparatus*.

THREE IN ONE

The artistic competition is divided into three parts — the team events, the individual combined events and the single apparatus events. In the team and combined competitions, the gymnasts perform on all the apparatus; in the single apparatus events, just one piece of equipment is used.

ON APPARATUS

Eight different kinds of apparatus are used in the 14 different artistic events. Men compete on six apparatus (pommel horse, rings, vault, parallel bars, horizontal bar and floor); the women on four (vault, uneven bars, balance beam and floor).

Alexei Nemov

SUPER STATS

Between 1956 and 1964, Larisa Latynina (URS) won 18 Olympic medals (including nine golds), making her the most successful competitor in Olympic history.

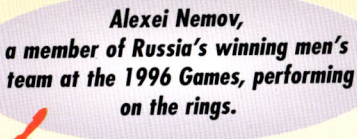

Alexei Nemov, a member of Russia's winning men's team at the 1996 Games, performing on the rings.

SCORING

All artistic gymnastic events are scored by two panels of judges. One panel is made up of two judges, who give each performance a score out of 10 for difficulty. The harder the moves attempted by the gymnast, the higher the score. The second panel, with six judges, assesses how well the moves were actually performed. They deduct points from the other panel's score for any mistakes and errors that the gymnast made.

Tatiana Gutsu

DID YOU KNOW?

The youngest-ever medallist in a gymnastic event was 10-year-old Dimitrios Loundras (GRE), who won a bronze medal on the parallel bars at the Games in 1896.

Since 1984, all male gymnasts must be 16 years old and female gymnasts at least 15.

The oldest person ever to win a medal in the gymnastics competition was 46-year-old Ethel Seymour (GBR), who won a bronze in 1928 in the women's team event.

A fraction of a point can make all the difference. In 1992, Tatiana Gutsu (EUN) beat Shannon Miller (USA) by just 0.012 points — the smallest-ever margin of victory in an Olympic gymnastic event!

DID YOU KNOW?

❓ In spite of suffering from a broken kneecap at the 1976 Games, Shun Fujimoto (JPN) managed to score 9.5 on the pommel horse and 9.7 on the rings – a personal best!

❓ Each country may enter one team and three individuals for each of the artistic events.

❓ The USSR won the women's team event eight times in a row from 1952–1980.

INDIVIDUAL CHAMPIONS

In the individual combined events gymnasts perform on all the apparatus, but compete on their own rather than as part of a team. The winners are known as the 'all-round' champions.

Each apparatus demands a different combination of strength, balance and agility. To become a combined champion like Li Xiaoshuang (CHN), gymnasts must master them all.

WHAT A HERO

If there was an Olympic medal for bravery, it would have been won by Shun Fujimoto (JPN) at the 1976 Games. Fujimoto broke his kneecap while competing in the men's team event. However, he knew that if he withdrew from the competition he would ruin his team's chances of winning a medal, so he kept his painful injury secret and went on to compete in two more events. Thanks to Fujimoto, Japan won the gold!

USA women's team, Atlanta 1996

TAKE A BOW

The USA women's team celebrate after winning the gold medal in front of their home crowd at the 1996 Games in Atlanta. It was the USA's first-ever victory in the women's team event.

REIGNING OLYMPIC CHAMPIONS: Men's team: RUSSIA / **Men's individual combined:** Li Xiaoshuang (CHN)

TEAM & COMBINED EVENTS

Li Xiaoshuang

In the team and individual combined events, competitors must perform on all the different apparatus.

EVERYTHING'S OPTIONAL!

Previously at the Olympics, the gymnasts had to perform twice on each apparatus. Once to do a compulsory routine that was set by the judges, the second time to do a freestyle routine which they had composed themselves. At the Games in Sydney, however, there will be no compulsory exercises apart from in the trampoline events.

TEAM TOTALS

Each team is made up of six gymnasts but only five perform on each apparatus. Gymnasts can be awarded a maximum of 10 points; only the top four scores are counted. As men compete on six apparatus and women on four, the highest possible final score is 240 points for the men's team and 160 for the women's team.

SUPER STATS

The former Soviet Union dominated the gymnastic events at the Games. Even though the USSR ceased to exist in 1991, it's still top of the medals table to this day. In fact, the USSR has more medals than its two closest rivals combined!

USSR – 204   Japan – 86   USA – 76

Women's team: USA / **Women's individual combined:** Lilia Podkopayeva (UKR)

SINGLE APPARATUS: FLOOR

The floor is the only single apparatus event in which men and women compete on the same apparatus in exactly the same way.

ANIMAL OLYMPIANS

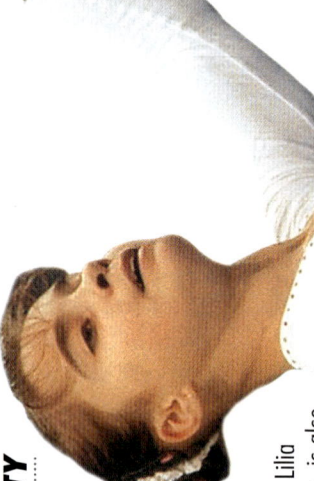

When it comes to performing magnificent jumps and twists, even an Olympic gymnast can't match a killer whale. These mighty mammals love showing off their acrobatic skills and can leap 6 metres out of the water.

SOME SOMERSAULT!

Vladimir Gogoladze (URS) turned Olympic gymnastics upside down during the floor exercises at the 1988 Games. To the amazement of the crowd and judges, he performed a spectacular triple somersault — the first in the history of the Games!

Vladimir Gogoladze

STAR QUALITY

The floor exercises test the four essential qualities that all great gymnasts need: flexibility, grace, strength and balance. The reigning Olympic women's champion, Lilia Podkopayeva (UKR), is also the reigning women's all-round champion.

REIGNING OLYMPIC CHAMPIONS: Men's event: Ioannis Melissanidis (GRE)

MAT FACTS

The floor exercises are performed on a 12 metre square mat made from a springy material suitable for both powerful take offs and soft landings. Around the edge of the mat is a 1 metre-wide safety border. Gymnasts must not step on the border except when approaching or leaving the mat.

ON THE FLOOR

In the floor exercises, gymnasts must perform a continuous series of acrobatic movements. These include somersaults, splits, tumbles, twists and handstands. In the women's event, each routine must last between 60 and 90 seconds. The men's routines must be between 50 and 70 seconds long.

DID YOU KNOW?

- The women's floor exercises are performed to music but the men's routines are not.
- In 1992, the women's floor exercises were won by Lavinia Milosovici (ROM) with a 'perfect 10' performance.
- Competitors are penalized if they finish their routine outside the time limits.

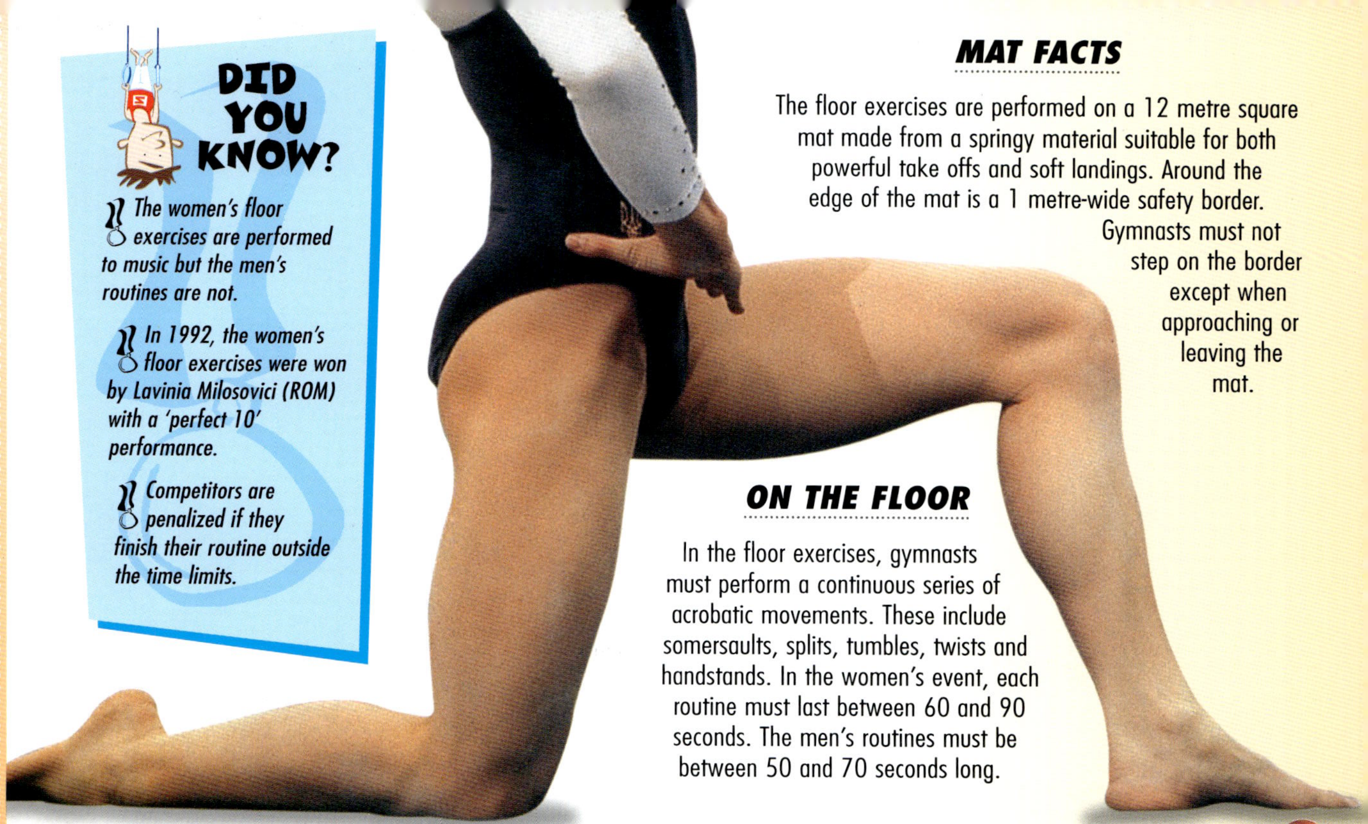

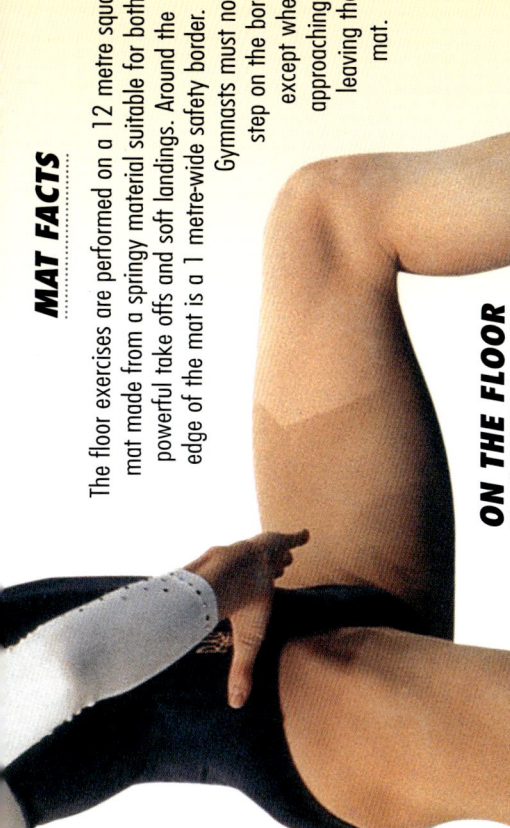

Lilia Podkopayeva

Women's event: Lilia Podkopayeva (UKR)

SINGLE APPARATUS: POMMEL HORSE

The pommel horse is a rectangular block on four legs which looks a bit like a headless horse – hence its name!

SADDLE UP!

The top of the horse is just over 1 metre high and 1.5 metres long, with two raised handles in the centre known as 'pommels'. Only men compete in this event.

Chalking hands to improve grip

SCISSOR LEGS

On the pommel horse, the gymnast must support his weight using his hands while he performs a series of continuous swinging movements with his legs. One move is known as the 'scissors'. Here the gymnast has one leg on either side of the horse. As he swings from side to side, he lets go with one hand and switches his legs. The leg at the front of the horse goes to the back and the leg at the back of the horse goes to the front.

SUPER STATS

How does the size of a pommel horse compare with the height of the back of a real horse?

Pommel horse – 105 cm high

The average horse – 150 cm high

The tallest horse – 175 cm high

The shortest breed of horse – 76 cm high

1996 OLYMPIC MEDALLISTS: GOLD: Li Donghua (SUI)

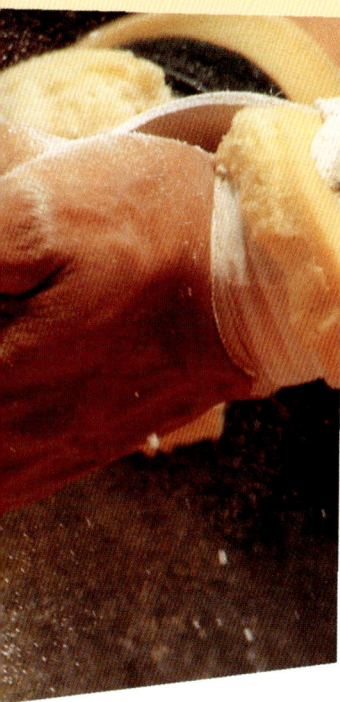

A DUSTING DOWN

Before performing on the horse, competitors dip their hands into a bowl of magnesium carbonate. This is a fine white powder which absorbs sweat and helps gymnasts to grip the pommels without their hands sticking or slipping.

DID YOU KNOW?

- The pommel horse is sometimes also called the side horse.

- Gymnasts are expected to use the whole length of the horse and to travel up and down it on their hands!

- Each country may enter no more than three competitors in the individual apparatus events.

Dimitry Bilozertchev

SHARING THE GLORY

There has been a triple tie for a gold medal on only two occasions at the Olympics and both were in the pommel horse event! In 1948, three Finnish gymnasts shared the gold. Forty years later, in 1988, Dimitry Bilozertchev (URS) shared the gold with the gymnasts from Bulgaria and Hungary.

SILVER: Marius Urzica (ROM) / **BRONZE**: Alexei Nemov (RUS)

Just before each performance, gymnasts coat the soles of their shoes in a sticky resin to prevent them from slipping.

Gymnasts on the bar are allowed to compete barefoot but most prefer to wear slippers.

Dominique Moceanu

Bandages are strapped around injured muscles and joints to provide support.

BALANCING ACT

Gymnasts must perform a routine lasting between 50 and 70 seconds on the narrow balance beam, without falling off! Competitors are expected to use the whole length of the beam and typical moves include jumps, leaps, running steps, turns, handsprings and somersaults. Only women compete in this event at the Games.

DID YOU KNOW?

- If a gymnast falls off the beam, she will automatically have 0.4 points deducted from her score.

- Gymnasts also have points deducted from their score if they behave in an unsporting manner.

- Coaches are forbidden to talk to their gymnasts while they are performing.

Gymnasts wear stretchy leotards that allow them to move freely.

Dominique Moceanu won a gold medal at the 1996 Games in the women's team event.

The beam is a horizontal wooden bar 1.2 metres above the ground. It is 10 metres long and just 10 cm wide.

1996 OLYMPIC MEDALLISTS: GOLD: Shannon Miller (USA)

SINGLE APPARATUS: BALANCE BEAM

Walking along the narrow balance beam looks hard enough – just imagine doing cartwheels and somersaults as well!

IT TAKES STYLE

On the beam, as with the other all-female events, balance and agility count for more than sheer strength. Artistry and a sense of style are also very important. This is because, in addition to looking at how well each individual move is executed, the judges also take into consideration the artistic effect of the performance as a whole.

ANIMAL OLYMPIANS

If there was a gold medal for balancing in the Animal Olympics, it would be won by a spider. Spiders can walk along a single strand of the silk which they use to build their webs – even though it's less than 1 mm wide!

Shannon Miller

The reigning Olympic champion in the balance beam event is Shannon Miller (USA).

SILVER: Lilia Podkopayeva (UKR) / **BRONZE:** Gina Gogean (ROM)

SINGLE APPARATUS: HORIZONTAL BAR

Competitors in the horizontal bar event really get things swinging at the Games!

WHAT A PERFORMANCE!

Competitors in this event grip the bar using either one or two hands but some of the most spectacular manoeuvres involve letting go completely, performing a twist or turn in the air then grabbing hold of the bar again. Only men compete in this event.

Gymnasts' trousers have foot straps to prevent the bottom of the trousers being pulled up.

Male gymnasts usually wear lightweight slippers, although they may compete barefoot if they prefer.

Most male gymnasts wear a simple, sleeveless vest.

Leather straps tied along the gymnast's hands support his wrist and help him to grip the bar.

ANIMAL OLYMPIANS

Gibbons are the greatest swingers in the animal kingdom. Using their long, powerful arms they cover more than 3 metres in a single swing!

1996 OLYMPIC MEDALLISTS: GOLD: Andreas Wecker (GER) / **SILVER:** Krasimir Douner

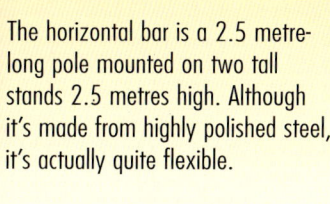
Andreas Wecker

POLE TO POLE

The horizontal bar is a 2.5 metre-long pole mounted on two tall stands 2.5 metres high. Although it's made from highly polished steel, it's actually quite flexible.

Andreas Wecker (GER) is the reigning Olympic champion.

Male gymnasts at the Games wear tight-fitting trousers made from an elasticated material.

GOLDEN BOY

Vitaly Scherbo (EUN/BLR) won six gold medals at the 1992 Games. In doing so, he set the record for the most gold medals ever won by a gymnast at one Games! At the 1996 Olympics he added three bronzes to his medal collection.

Vitaly Scherbo

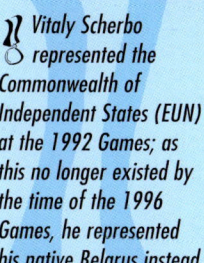

DID YOU KNOW?

- Vitaly Scherbo represented the Commonwealth of Independent States (EUN) at the 1992 Games; as this no longer existed by the time of the 1996 Games, he represented his native Belarus instead.

- Nobody knows the name of the gymnast who won the bronze medal on the horizontal bar at the 1896 Games!

- The men's gymnastic events used to include a rope climbing race. This was held for the last time in 1932.

BRONZE: Vitaly Scherbo (BLR), Fan Bin (CHN) and Alexei Nemov (RUS)

Li Lu (CHN)

DID YOU KNOW?

♫ The uneven bars are also known as the asymmetrical bars.

♫ Competitors on the horizontal and uneven bars must keep moving all the time — they are not allowed to come to a stop.

♫ At 2.45 metres high the tallest of the two bars is about twice as tall as an average seven-year-old!

Hands and fingers in a graceful pose

Arms outstretched

Chest thrust outwards

Feet together

HAPPY LANDINGS

In all the artistic events (apart from the floor events), the gymnasts must 'dismount' (jump off the apparatus) at the end of their routines. Competitors try to make their dismounts as spectacular as possible by flinging themselves into the air for a grand finale of somersaults and twists. All dismounts must end with the gymnast in the finish position, shown right.

1996 OLYMPIC MEDALLISTS: GOLD: Svetlana Chorkina (RUS)

SINGLE APPARATUS: UNEVEN BARS

While men perform on a single horizontal bar, women gymnasts have not one but two bars to contend with!

THE SECOND PARALLEL

The uneven parallel bars is an event for women gymnasts only. The apparatus consists of two horizontal poles set at different heights with a gap between them. The taller pole is 2.45 metres above the ground while the lower one is 1.65 metres high (an average nine-year-old, standing on tiptoe, would just be able to reach it).

BAR-ILLIANT!

This event is similar to the men's horizontal bar, except that the gymnast performs on two bars. Competitors swing over, under and around each of the bars, constantly switching from one to the other while performing difficult manoeuvres including pikes, tucks and twists. This picture shows the reigning Olympic champion, Svetlana Chorkina (RUS), in action.

Svetlana Chorkina

SUPER STATS

The former Soviet Union is top of the league in the uneven bars event with three golds. Next are China, East Germany and Hungary who have each won two golds.

SILVER: Bi Wengji (CHN) and Amy Chow (USA) / **BRONZE:** No bronze was awarded because there were two silver medallists.

SINGLE APPARATUS: RINGS

The rings event is the supreme test of strength. But muscle power alone isn't enough – control and grace are needed, too!

Yuri Chechi (ITA)

RINGING ROUND

This event is for men only and is performed on two rings suspended from cables about 2.5 metres above the floor. Gymnasts must keep the rings as still as possible while performing their routine. It requires tremendous physical strength – just take a look at the bulging biceps of Italian gymnast Yuri Chechi!

ANIMAL OLYMPIANS

Routines on the rings last less than 5 minutes but bats hang upside down for most of the day. They even sleep in this position!

1996 OLYMPIC MEDALLISTS: GOLD: Yuri Chechi (ITA)

Yik Siang Loke

NEED A LIFT?

On the rings and the horizontal bar, a coach or team-mate may lift the competitor up so that he can reach the apparatus. This is the only occasion where a gymnast is allowed to receive help without being penalized.

HOLD STILL

Routines on the rings usually include a number of holding moves in which the competitor remains perfectly still for 3 seconds. One of the most difficult is known as the cross — gymnasts move their bodies in an upright position with their arms out sideways. In this picture, Yik Siang Loke (MAS) shows how it's done!

SAFETY FIRST

In addition to the rubber safety mats which are placed underneath the rings, people known as 'spotters' are positioned nearby. Their job is to try to catch the gymnast if he falls. However, a competitor who receives help from a spotter automatically has 0.4 points deducted from his score.

DID YOU KNOW?

- Rubber safety mats are used in all the artistic events apart from the floor.

- At the Games in 1952, gymnasts from the Soviet Union won gold, silver and bronze medals on the rings.

- In 1912 and 1920, the Games included a team event for men known as the 'Swedish system'. On both occasions it was won by Sweden!

SILVER: Szilveszter Csollany (HUN) / **BRONZE:** Dan Burnica (ROM)

SINGLE APPARATUS: VAULT

The vault is an event for both men and women – but they use the apparatus very differently!

SPOT THE DIFFERENCE

Both men and women compete in the vault, using the same equipment. However, men vault across the horse's length while women jump across it sideways. Also, the horse used in the men's event is 10 cm higher than the one used by women.

DID YOU KNOW?

- Competitors in the men's event must touch the horse as they jump over it; this rule does not apply in the women's event.
- Gymnasts are judged from the moment they step out to perform, including the run up to the vault.
- In 1980, Aleksandr Dityatin (URS) became the first man ever to score a perfect 10 at the Olympics.

Alexei Nemov (RUS)

The horse is positioned lengthways in the men's event.

REIGNING OLYMPIC CHAMPIONS: Men's event: Alexei Nemov (RUS)

JUMP FOR IT

In this event, competitors use a bouncy springboard to jump over a vault, which is like the pommel horse only without the handles. As the gymnasts fly through the air, they perform spectacular twist and turns — and even spin themselves upside down!

Competitors in the vault event are allowed a run up. The runway must be 1 metre wide and 25 metres long.

By leaping onto this springboard in front of the vault, the competitors catapult themselves into the air.

Henrietta Onodi (HUN)

A SECOND GO

The women's vault is the only gymnastic event at the Olympics in which competitors perform twice on the apparatus. The gymnast's final score is the average score from both attempts. Men, on the other hand, only perform once.

ANIMAL OLYMPIANS

When it comes to vaulting at the Animal Olympics, frogs would leap at the chance to win a gold medal. African sharp-nosed frogs can vault across more than 5 metres — that's longer than a family car.

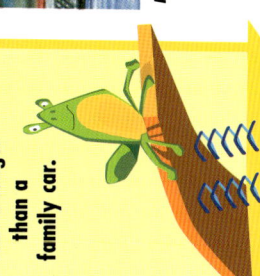

Women's event: Simona Amanar (ROM)

SINGLE APPARATUS: PARALLEL BARS

The parallel bars event demands the strength of the rings and the agility of the horizontal bar.

Nikolay Andrianov

GOLDEN GREAT

Nikolay Andrianov (URS) holds the record for the most medals ever won by a male competitor in any sport at the Olympic Games. Between 1972 and 1980 he won no less than 15 medals in gymnastic events, including a silver on the parallel bars in 1976. He also shares the record for being the most successful male gymnast, having won six gold medals.

SUPER STATS

Japan and the USSR head the medals table in this event, both having won it four times. Switzerland has three victories, while the USA and Germany have each won two gold medals.

1996 OLYMPIC MEDALLISTS: GOLD: Rustam Sharipov (UKR)

AGILITY & STRENGTH

The gymnasts demonstrate their agility and balance by performing twists, handstands and swinging moves on the bars. They also perform holding moves and other moves which are done very slowly. These are designed to show off their strength and control.

RAIL WAY

The two wooden rails used in this event are both 1.75 metres high and about 0.5 metres apart. Competitors must support their weight using only their arms. This requires mega muscle power, which is why the parallel bars is another men-only event.

During a holding move the gymnast must remain completely still. Vitaly Scherbo (EUN), who won the gold in 1992, makes it look easy here but this move takes great strength and concentration.

Vitaly Scherbo (EUN)

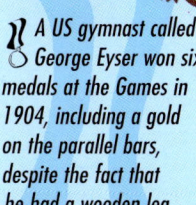

DID YOU KNOW?

A US gymnast called George Eyser won six medals at the Games in 1904, including a gold on the parallel bars, despite the fact that he had a wooden leg.

The first-ever gymnastics gold medal was awarded to the German team, who won the parallel bars event in 1896.

In 1972, all the medals for the parallel bars were won by Japanese gymnasts.

SILVER: Jair Lynch (USA) / **BRONZE:** Vitaly Scherbo (BLR)

DID YOU KNOW?

- In 1988, Marina Lobatch (URS) won the individual gold medal after scoring a perfect 10 in every single one of her routines.

- In the early 1900s, rhythmic gymnastics was known as 'modern gymnastics'.

- Rhythmic gymnastics made its first apparance at the games in 1984.

The two clubs are bottle-shaped with a thick end and a thin end. They must be the same length and weigh 150 g.

The ball measures 19–20 cm across. It can be made of either rubber or soft plastic and must weigh 400 g.

The rope must be made from hemp or a similar material. The length of the rope used depends on the height of the gymnast.

The hoop must weigh at least 300 g and measure 80–90 cm across. It can be made of either wood or plastic.

The ribbon is made from a strip of material 7 metres long, attached to a short stick, 50–60 cm long, which the competitor holds.

IN CONTACT

The gymnast's performance must end precisely on the last note of the music. At the end of her routine, the gymnast must be touching the apparatus, although she can use any part of the body she likes.

Alina Stoica (ROM)

1996 OLYMPIC MEDALLISTS: GOLD: Yekaterina Serebryanskaya (UKR)

RHYTHMIC: INDIVIDUAL

Unlike artistic gymnastics, all the events in rhythmic gymnastics are for women only.

ROUTINE WORK

In rhythmic gymnastics, the routines are always accompanied by music and many of the steps and movements performed by the competitors actually come from ballet. The gymnasts must keep the apparatus moving all the time and each routine must last between 75 and 90 seconds. A penalty of 0.05 points is deducted for every second a gymnast performs over or under this time limit.

LEARN THE LINGO

These ballet terms are also used in rhythmic gymnastics:

Plié – a knee-bending movement

Jeté – jumping from one leg to another

Arabesque – standing on one leg with the other held out at a right angle

Attitude – standing on one leg with the other held out backwards with the knee bent

SPOT THE DIFFERENCE

The difference between artistic and rhythmic gymnastics is simple — rhythmic gymnastics are performed with an apparatus, rather than on one. In the individual event each gymnast performs four times, each time with a different piece of apparatus. There are five altogether: a ball, a rope, a ribbon, a pair of clubs and a hoop.

SILVER: Yanina Batyrchina (RUS) / **BRONZE:** Yelena Vitrichenko (UKR)

RHYTHMIC: TEAM

Diana Popova (BUL)

A team event in the rhythmic gymnastics competition was introduced at the 1996 Olympics.

TEAM WORK

Each team is made up of five gymnasts who perform on the mat together. Every team does two different routines. In the first routine, all the gymnasts perform using clubs; in the second, two team members use hoops while the other three use ribbons.

WINNING RIBBONS

Competitors performing with the ribbon must keep the material in constant, fluid motion throughout the performance. One of the most impressive and daring moves involves throwing the ribbon up high into the air then dancing across the mat and catching it as it falls to the ground.

SUPER STATS

The ribbon used by gymnasts in rhythmic events is about three times as long as an elephant's trunk!

1996 OLYMPIC MEDALLISTS: GOLD: SPAIN

THREE-WAY SCORING

Rhythmic gymnasts are scored by three panels of judges (not two as is the case in artistic events). Here's how the scoring works:

1) The 'technical' panel award up to four points (five in the individual event) according to the difficulty of the routine.
2) The 'artistic' panel award up to six points (up to five in the individual event) for the beauty and originality of the performance.
3) The 'execution' panel award up to 10 points according to how well each move is performed — the more mistakes they spot, the lower the gymnasts' score.

DID YOU KNOW?

- Rhythmic gymnastics are performed on a mat 13 metres square surrounded by a 1 metre safety area.

- In the team event, each score is out of 20; in the individual event, the points awarded by the judges are halved to give a score out of 10.

- At the 1996 Games the Spanish beat the Bulgarian team into second place by just 0.067 points!

Yelena Vitrichenko (UKR)

BEND & STRETCH

Rhythmic gymnasts bend over backwards to please the judges — quite literally! In most routines, you'll see incredible stretches and other moves designed to show off the flexibility and suppleness of the gymnast's body.

SILVER: BULGARIA / **BRONZE:** RUSSIA

DID YOU KNOW?

- The bed on a trampoline is just 6 mm thick!
- Every routine performed in the trampoline events must contain 10 recognized moves.
- The first purpose-built modern trampoline was built in the 1930s.

A padded safety platform helps to protect competitors who accidentally bounce off.

Markings on the trampoline help the competitor to land on the centre of the bed.

The springy part of the trampoline is called the 'bed'. It's made of a material, usually nylon, which is both strong and stretchy.

Trampoline

The bed is stretched across a strong metal frame 5.05 metres long and 2.91 metres wide.

THE BOUNCIEST NATIONS

As trampolining is a new Olympic sport, there aren't any reigning Olympic champions. The three top teams to watch out for at Sydney are Russia, Germany and Great Britain.

ROUND & ROUND

The trampolining events consist of two rounds. The first is a qualifying round in which each competitor must perform two routines. The first routine is compulsory (the moves are set by the judges and must be performed in order); the second routine is optional (competitors decide which moves they will perform and in which order). The second round decides the medals and consists of one optional routine only.

Trampolining is a new Olympic event.

TRAMPOLINE

At the Sydney Olympics there will be two events, one for men and one for women.

BOUNCING THROUGH HISTORY

The trampoline is named after a French circus performer, called Du Trampoline, who lived about 200 years ago. Apparently, he came up with the idea of using the safety net from the circus high wire act to bounce up and down while performing acrobatics.

Ian Ross (GBR)

Competitors wear the same clothes as other gymnasts, together with socks or gym shoes.

The bed of the trampoline is raised 1.15 metres off the ground.

SUPER STATS

Trampolinists can bounce up to 6 metres in the air — that's like jumping over a giraffe!

This means there will be no Olympic champions until the 2000 Games.

TRAMPOLINE (CONTINUED)

If the trampoline is a success at the Sydney Games, a team event could soon be on the Olympic programme, too.

Like other gymnastic events, trampolinists are awarded marks according to the difficulty of the moves they attempt and how well they perform them. Seven judges score each routine: two judges award points for difficulty while the other five score the execution of each move. The maximum score for a faultless performance is usually around 45 points.

ANIMAL OLYMPIANS

When it comes to bouncing, nothing can beat the klipspringer. This amazing African antelope can jump more than 7 metres into the air – which beats even an Olympic trampolinist!

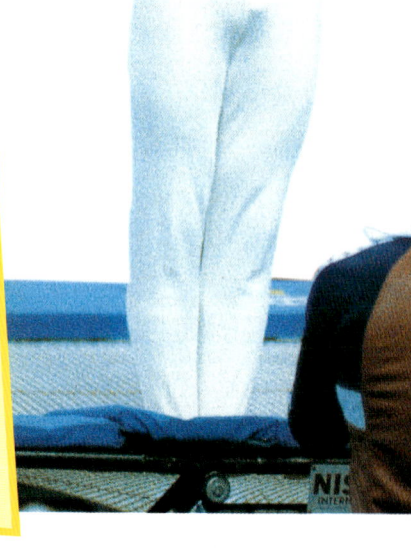

Finishing position

Trampolining is a new Olympic event.